To Ross,
who is young at heart!
With many blessings!
Rita Berglund

Rita Berglund

Written by
Rita Berglund

Cover design and photography by
Katy Tartakoff
of
The Children's Legacy

Artwork by
Laurie Shields

Published by
The Children's Legacy
P.O. Box 300305
Denver, CO 80203
303.830.7595

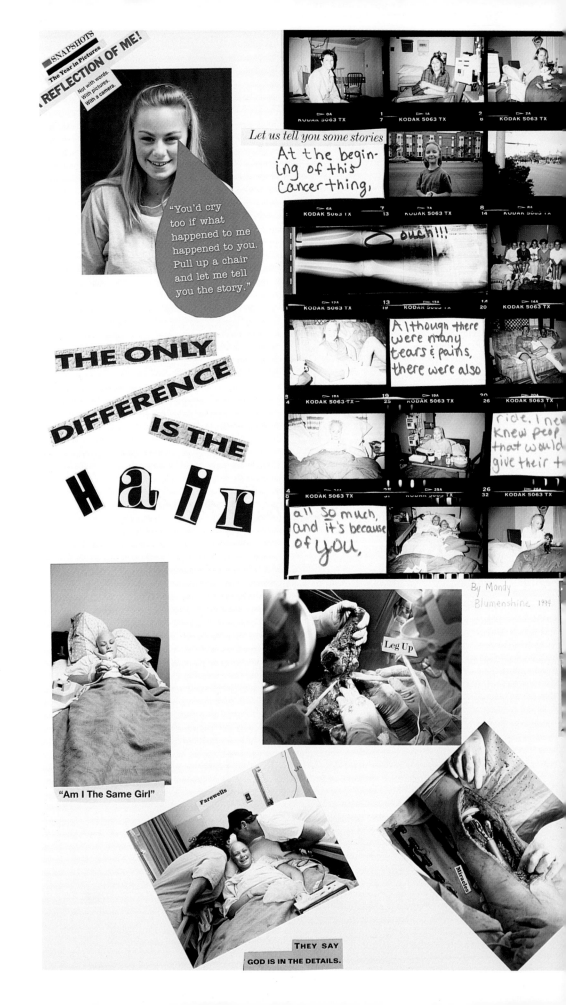

SNAPSHOTS
The Year in Pictures
A REFLECTION OF ME!
Not with words.
With pictures.
With a camera.

"You'd cry too if what happened to me happened to you. Pull up a chair and let me tell you the story."

THE ONLY DIFFERENCE IS THE Hair

Let us tell you some stories

At the beginning of this cancer thing,

ouch!!!

Although there were many tears & pains, there were also

ride. I new knew peop that would give their t

all so much, and it's because of you,

By Mandy Blumenshine 1994

Leg Up

"Am I The Same Girl"

Farewells

Miracles

THEY SAY GOD IS IN THE DETAILS.

Chemo Bear!

I was very scared & alone. I couldn't

THANKS A BUNCH!

Friends believe such a horrible thing could happen to any child. But it does, and it's very frightening.

many times of joy & happiness. I have so many people that have cared enough to stay with me along this roller coaster

and energy to share with someone with "cancer." But I love you

I've made it through!

Remember, Every picture has a story.

Family Circle

?

dance?

Me?

AN ALPHABET ABOUT KIDS WITH CANCER is brought to you by The Children's Legacy. The Children's Legacy has grown out of an urgent need in our society to communicate more openly about childhood illness, dying, and death. Children and adults alike have dreams as well as hopes of making a difference in life, however long or short

that life may be. We are a society in which people with d i f f e r e n c e s of any kind are taunted, teased, and d i s c r i m i n a t e d against.

The Children's Legacy embraces and celebrates differences! With the use of black and white photographs taken by nationally renowned photographer Katy Tartakoff, children learn to see their strengths, their beauty, their courage. Children and adults are challenged to look beyond the illness, the scars, the bald heads, the wheelchairs, and look instead at the essence of the human spirit.

An integral part of The Children's Legacy is a process of journaling in interactive workbooks called *MY STUPID ILLNESS, LET ME SHOW YOU MY WORLD,* and *BURNED AND BEAUTIFUL.* Children and family members create a legacy of their lives. If the child lives, photographs, journals, and other art forms can serve as a record of what the child transcended. If the child dies, his/her family has the journal and other tangible creations of art as a keepsake that remain a testimony to the child's life.

As with all The Children's Legacy programs, *AN ALPHABET ABOUT KIDS WITH CANCER* was created as a tool to assist children and their families in openly communicating about their most sacred thoughts as they heal into wellness or into death. The book was inspired by the spirit of children who live with cancer every day.

The author, Rita Berglund, is a wife and mother who experienced cancer firsthand when her son, Brandon, was diagnosed in 1989 with a malignant brain tumor (ependymoma). Years of treatment have brought hope and an urgency to communicate honestly about the power and diversity of our lives.

Added to the gift and grace of Rita's prose and Katy's photographs was the ability of Laurie Shields, artist extraordinaire, to illustrate the letters

and to direct the final design of the book. Laurie, an artist working with Droy Advertising, expertly expresses her child spirit through her illustrations.

IN LOVING MEMORY

JINNA MCPHERSON

Support for the publication of this book was provided with love by the family of Jinna McPherson.

Jinna was born September 25, 1983, in South Korea. Shortly thereafter, her father died, leaving Jinna, her mother and grandmother. Jinna's early recollection was that much of her time was spent with her grandmother. Jinna's mother apparently had little or no income so, realizing that she could not afford Jinna's education, which is required of parents in Korea, she offered three-year-old Jinna to an orphanage. After living there for a few months, Jinna was matched with the McPherson family and then flown to the US to become a daughter for Lynne and Gene and a sister for Heather.

Jinna arrived in Sturgis, South Dakota, at age four. She was soon enrolled in preschool and progressed through the third grade. At age five, Jinna began Suzuki violin, joining her sister Heather. She participated in six annual Suzuki Violin Institutes in Missoula, Montana, in the summers. She also won various awards for reading mastery.

When Jinna was diagnosed with a malignant brain tumor, she thought she would be sent back to Korea. Of course, she was not and, as a result, she felt like she was really part of the family for the first time.

After battling her cancer for about 18 months under the loving care of Denver physicians, Larry McCleary and Edward Arenson and their staffs, she died at home on November 24, 1993.

We, the parents and sister of Jinna, know that your child is as important and special to you as Jinna is to us. This is not a monument to Jinna but a way for us, in our grief, to offer each of you something we can all share repeatedly over the years, whenever necessary. In the business of cancer, virtually every help is needed, sooner or later, so use this when you need to but when you don't, remember where you left it.

I dedicate this book to Brianna, who thanks
God every night for her brother, Brandon,
and prays "that no more kids
will ever have cancer."

Rita

To the following bicyclists who supported
the birthing of this book, we give our
eternal thanks: Mike Boggess,
Bill Lugsch, Bill Robinson, Jim Swaim,
John Taylor, Ed Wolph.

Much love and appreciation to the
National Childhood Cancer Foundation
and all the children and families who were
kind enough to let us include their
photographs in this book.

And to all children and families around
the world living with a life-challenging
illness, our prayers are with you.

Rita and Katy

TABLE OF CONTENTS

A is for Aches

B is for Body

C is for Cancer

D is for Dying

E is for Exceptional

F is for Feelings

G is for Guilt

H is for Healing

I is for Intensive Care

J is for Joy

K is for Kids

L is for Living

M is for Medicine

N is for Needles

O is for Operation

P is for Parents

Q is for Quiet

R is for Radiation

S is for Siblings

T is for Transfusion

U is for Understanding

V is for Visualize

W is for Wishes

X is for X-Rays

Y is for Yo-Yo

Z is for Zowee!

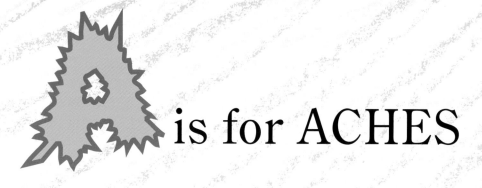# is for ACHES

Aches can be unusual things.

They can start out q u i e t l y.
They can start out quietly and
get louder
and louder.
So loud that we can't pretend them away.

Some aches come and go,
come and go,
come and go.
Some aches come hard
and fast
and wake you up!
Some aches are so bad that
you want to hold very, very still.

Aches can ruin your play,
can ruin your day.

Aches can send you to your mom and dad
and to your doctor…

Aaaah!
Why are there aches?
Why do I ache?

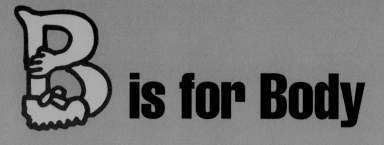

B is for Body

This is my body.
These are my hands,
        this is my head,
                and my feet,
                        and my all in between.

My body is a growing place,
        a place of stories,
                a place of dances and games,
                        singing and laughing,
                                feeling and thinking,
                                        a place of doing and being,
                                waking and sleeping,
                        healing and hurting.

Hurting, aching —
        that is what is happening now.

Something is somehow wrong.
        The doctors are looking,
                listening,
                        probing,
                                poking,
                                        asking questions.

But Hey! Be Careful.
This is My Body!!!!!!!!!!!!!!!

C IS FOR CANCER

The doctor says I have cancer.
I'm not sure what that means.
It's something about cells
      and the way they grow inside my body.

Everyone seems very, very sad.
Why do I have cancer?
I know I didn't catch it like a cold.
I know I didn't cause it by doing something bad.
I know I didn't get it from someone else.
So why do I have cancer?

No one really knows.
No one can really answer that question.
The only thing I know is that
I have cancer.

Now I will have to
learn a lot of new things —
**new things about cancer and
new things about me.**

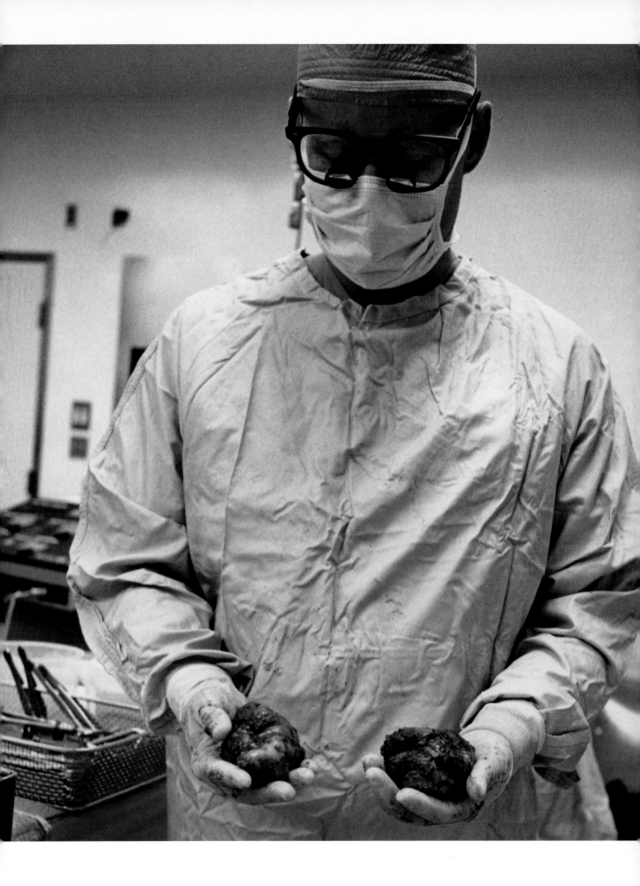

D IS FOR DYING

Am I going to die?

When you find out that you have cancer
one of the first things
you may want to know is,
"Am I going to die?"
Moms and dads think about it.
Grandmas and grandpas think about it.
Brothers and sisters think about it.
And kids who have cancer think about it.

No one really knows the answer.
But it can be a good thing to talk about.
Talking about it can sometimes help you
find more courage. . .
and give more courage away.

What do you think dying is like?
Have you ever known anyone who died?
Have you ever been with someone
who was dying?

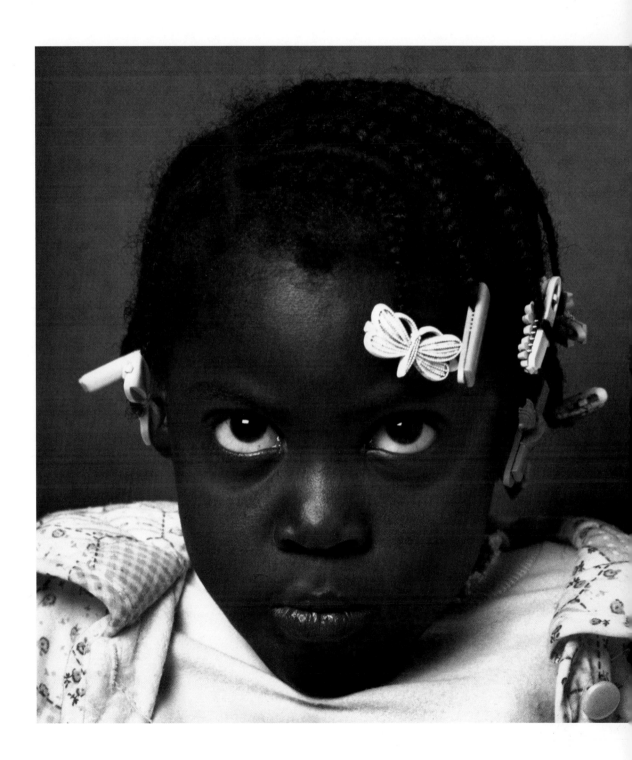

IS FOR EXCEPTIONAL

Exceptional is a long word that means
"out of the ordinary"
or "remarkable."
When you have cancer, you meet a lot of
exceptional people.
You meet doctors
who want to make the cancer go away.
They are exceptional.
You meet nurses who want to take care of you.
They are exceptional.
You also meet lots of other people
who want to help you and be your friend.
They are exceptional, too.

And kids.
Other kids get cancer.
They are very exceptional.
So when you have cancer
you have lots and lots of
exceptional friends
and meet lots and lots of
exceptional people.

Because – YOU ARE EXCEPTIONAL!

F is for Feelings

When you have cancer,
        you have lots of feelings.

Sometimes there are so many feelings,
    it is difficult to sort them out.

There is anger and sadness.
There are scared feelings and mad feelings,
    lost and lonely feelings.
Sometimes you feel crazy, and you
    laugh or yell.
There are hope feelings.
    Joy feelings. Tears. Hugs.
        Give up and hide feelings.
    Jump and be strong feelings.

Feelings are like crayons —
    they come in all kinds of colors.

Find someone special,
        and tell them about your feelings,
because FEELINGS ARE IMPORTANT!

G IS FOR GUILT

Guilt is a feeling that no one likes.

When someone has cancer,
guilt is a feeling that many people feel.

Moms and dads sometimes wonder
if they did something that caused the cancer.
They feel guilty when the cancer and
the medical treatments hurt the person they love.

Sometimes brothers and sisters wonder
if they did something to cause the cancer.

Sometimes grandpas and grandmas wonder.

Sometimes kids with cancer wonder.

Cancer is no one's fault.
Cancer is no one's fault.
Cancer is no one's fault!

Forgiveness and understanding
are more helpful than guilt.

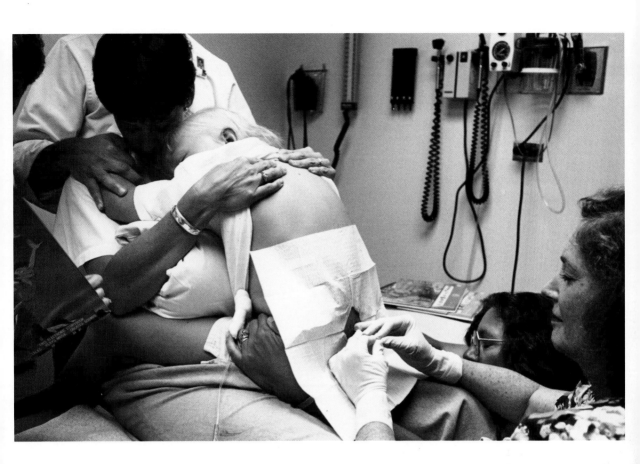

 IS FOR HEALING

When someone we love has cancer,
    we want a cure, we want healing.
People with cancer work hard.
    They take medicine and may go through
        procedures that are painful or uncomfortable.

Many times the cure comes —
    more and more kids go on to
        a long life without cancer.

Healing can happen
    even when there is no cure.
Healing is about all of us —
    our emotions,
        our souls,
           our spirits,
                our thoughts,
                    our actions . . .

Healing is hard work.
Healing involves all the people you love
    and care about.

Sometimes we find healing
    in our life and our living.
Sometimes healing can only fully come
    in the miracle of death.

What does healing mean to you?

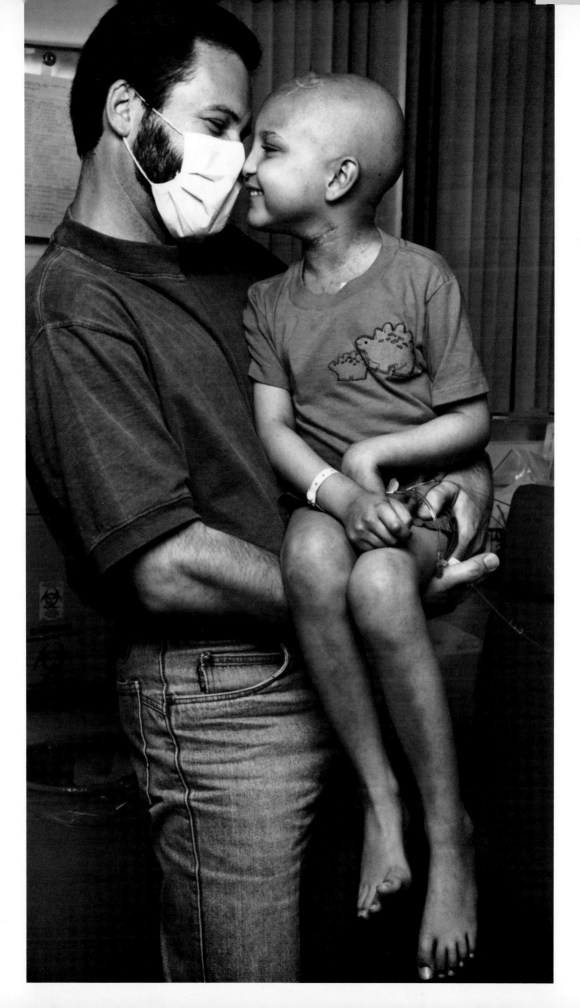

 **IS FOR INTENSIVE CARE**

When you need a lot of healing,
        you need intensive care.

There is even a special place in the hospital
        called the Intensive Care Unit.

It is a special room
        where nurses and doctors stay near you . . .

near you every minute of the day and night.

Others who love you may also stay near.

The room is often full of special machines
        (which are usually noisy)
           and special people
              (who are usually quiet).

All together, everyone is working very hard
        to help you get well and feel better.

Sometimes hospitals call the Intensive Care Unit the "ICU."

    "ICU" can also mean —

        "**I C**are about **YOU!**"

Have you ever been in an Intensive Care Unit?

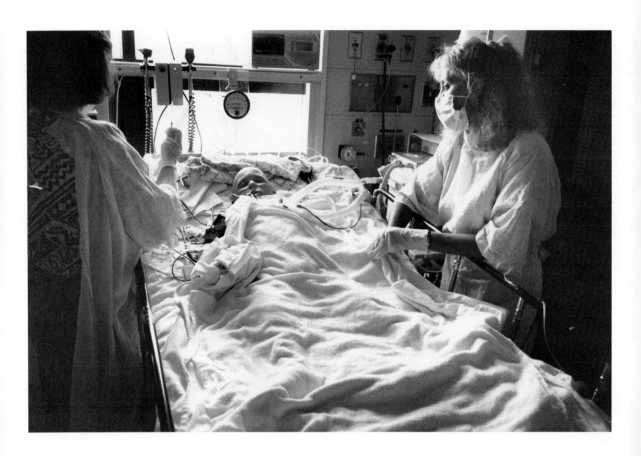

J IS FOR JOY

Who is going to argue?
Life with cancer is very hard.
So when good things happen
you learn about joy.
Joy — that deep down happy, healing,
look out world, watch me now,
kind of feeling!
Often it is the simple things that bring me joy:
    the smile from a visiting clown.
    having a water fight.
    getting a hug from someone I love.
    friends coming to visit me at the hospital.
    having a big bowl of ice cream at midnight.
    getting to go to school.

What are some of the things that bring you joy?

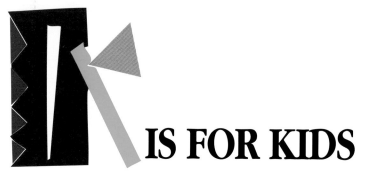 **IS FOR KIDS**

There are kids who have cancer
    and kids who don't.
There are kids with red hair
    and kids with black hair.
There are kids with handicaps
    and kids with no handicaps.
There are kids good at math
    and kids good at art.
There are kids good at jumping
    and kids good at singing.

Every kid is unique and special.
Yet all kids,
    all kids have some things in common.
There are some things
    that even cancer doesn't change.

Do you know what they are?
What are you good at?
What things are difficult for you?

L IS FOR LIVING

I am alive!
    I am alive!
        I am a life!
            And I have a life!

Having cancer is a part of who I am, yes.
But it is only a part.
        I am still a kid.
I am still busy living and just being me.
I still like ice cream and baseball.
I want to hear your jokes
        and go play at your house.
I like parties and escalators and phone calls.
I like to show friends my collections
        and talk about summer vacations.
Who I am hasn't changed.
        Hello, it's still me.

        I have a life! Do you?

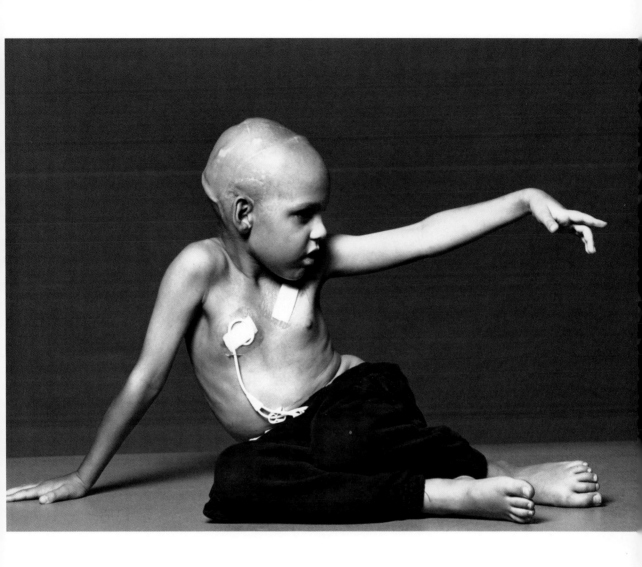

IS FOR MEDICINE

When you have cancer
> you have to take many different kinds of medicine.

There are
> pills that you swallow,
> pills that you chew,
> stuff that you drink,
> stuff that you spit,
> stuff that goes in through a tube,
> stuff that tastes awful,
> stuff that tastes good,
> stuff that looks pink or red or yellow or . . . ?

Sometimes it is hard
> to take so much medicine. (Yuck!!!)

But remember,
> someday you may be better,
>> and you won't need so much medicine.

Do you take lots of medicine?

> What kinds do you have to take?

> What is the medicine for?

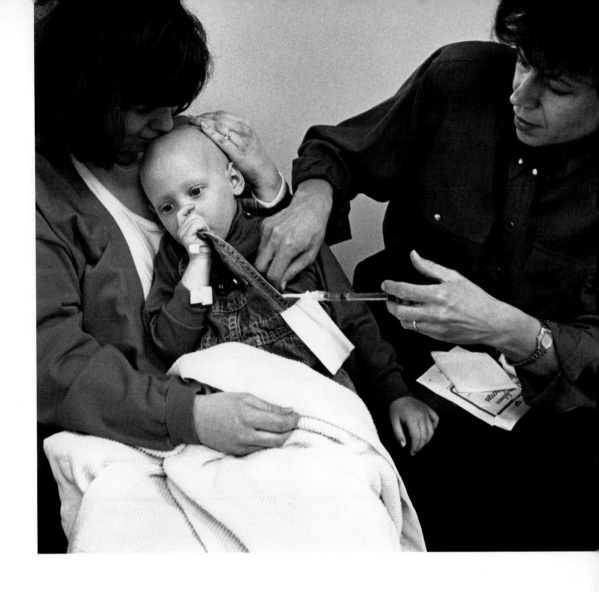

 **IS FOR NEEDLES**

Unfortunately, some medicines can only be given
through a syringe and needle.
    And I don't know about you,
        but needles sometimes
            scare me.

Kids often call these injections "pokes."

When you have cancer,
    you see lots of needles for giving pokes.
You have to get
    "pokes" for medicine and
    "pokes" for IVs (Into your Veins stuff.)
    "pokes" for spinal taps
    "pokes" for drawing out blood samples.

The hurt from the needle only lasts a short while —
    that's the good thing.

The other good thing is this,
    if your doctors know you are going to be
        getting lots of these pokes,
            they will talk to you about some
                fancy ways to make the pokes easier.
Great idea, huh!

Do you get lots of pokes with needles?

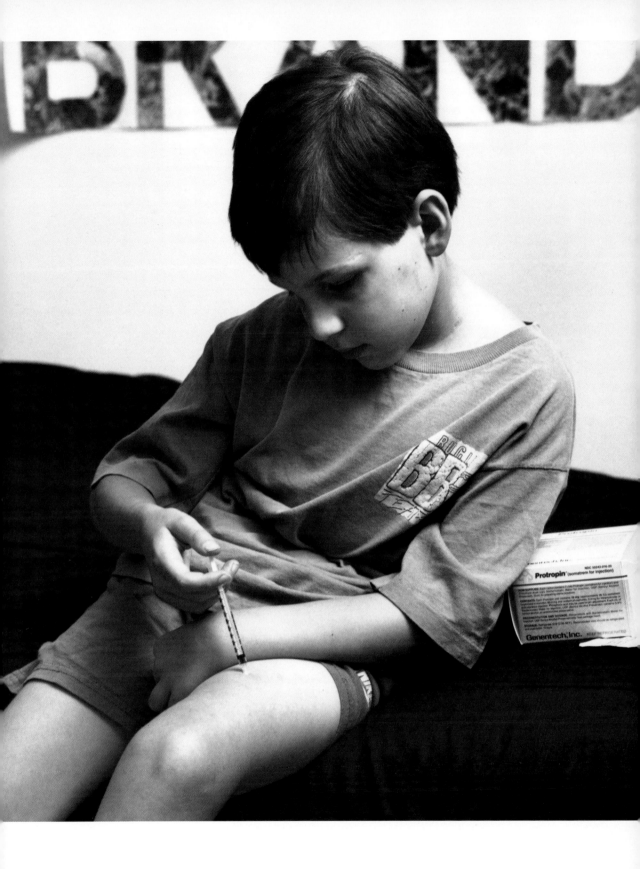

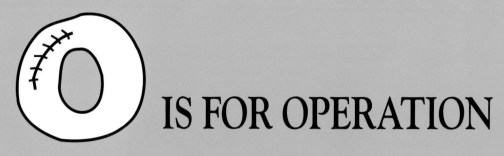 IS FOR OPERATION

Sometimes medicine is not enough,
    and you may need an operation.
Operations are also called "surgery."
There are many different reasons for operations.
If your doctors think you need an operation or surgery
    they will talk to you and your parents.
Special doctors, called anesthesiologists,
    will also talk to you.
The anesthesiologist knows about special medicine that
    will let you sleep during the operation
    so you don't feel any pain.

Doctors can accomplish some pretty wonderful things
    during an operation.

Have you ever had an operation?

What was it like?

Do you know anyone else who has had an operation?

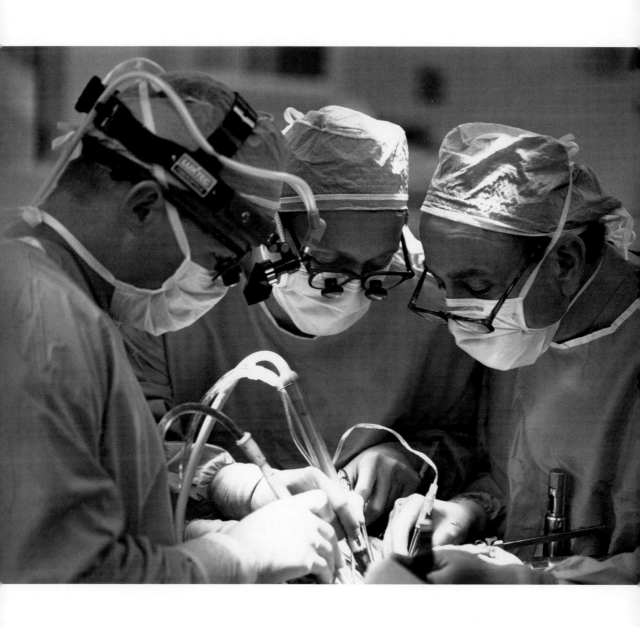

P IS FOR PARENTS
(and pig pile!)

Parents' best dreams and hopes are
expressed in their children.

So parents are very sad and scared
when they find out that
one of their kids has cancer.

They have to learn a lot
so they will know how
to give medical care and
so they can work
to get the best treatment and
the best help.

Being a parent is tough work.

**But loving children is immensely,
gigantically, enormously, irrevocably,
the best!!**

IS FOR QUIET

When you have cancer
    some people get very quiet.
They don't know what to say.
They are trying to care.
But having someone they love with cancer
    may be a new experience.
So be patient with them.
When it is too quiet
    you can remind people how important
        it is just to share how they feel.
You can also remind them that you are still
    a kid and still like to have fun.

Yes, there are times to be quiet
    and there are times to be —

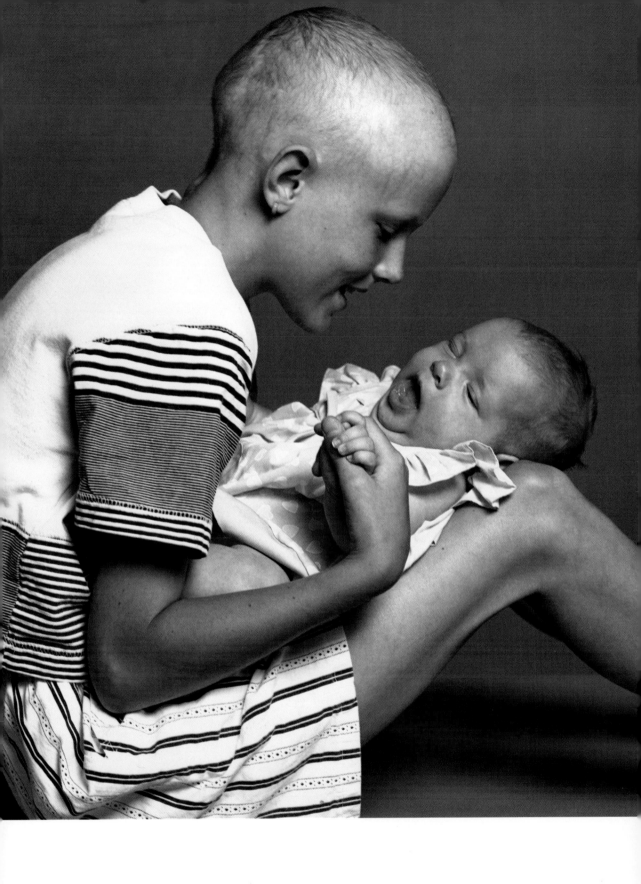

 **IS FOR RADIATION**

Some kinds of cancer
    are treated with radiation.

Radiation is like an invisible beam of light
        or energy that goes inside you.

The radiation treatment doesn't hurt
    and usually doesn't take very long.

Radiation is strong medicine.
        Although the treatment itself doesn't hurt,
            you may feel and see some unpleasant
                changes that it causes
                    in your body.

Some kinds of radiation are very complicated.
        Like all cancer treatments,
            doctors and researchers are always looking for
                new and better ways to cure cancer.

Have you ever been treated with radiation?

What was it like?

What happened when the treatments were finished?

IS FOR SIBLINGS

Brothers and sisters are siblings.
Sisters and sisters are siblings.
Brothers and brothers are siblings.

Sometimes dads and moms have siblings.
Sometimes grandpas and grandmas have siblings.
Do you have any siblings?

Did you know that it is hard and scary for a sibling
to see a brother or sister hurt?
It is hard when they don't get to help.
It is hard when they are left out or left behind.
It is hard when no one asks how they are.
It is hard when no one brings them presents or sends them cards.

It can be very, very hard.
But keep them close.
They are important.

They know how much you may need to play.
They may know some secret ways to cheer you on,
or brighten a difficult day.

Siblings are Special
and can be a great Support.

Hurray for Siblings!
P.S. If you need to — adopt some.

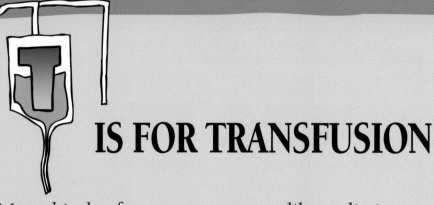# IS FOR TRANSFUSION

Many kinds of cancer treatments like radiation and chemotherapy can make it difficult for our bodies to create enough blood cells. When this happens, you may need a transfusion of blood or blood products that are donated by someone else. This is a wonderful way that others share their life and energy with you.

T is also for transplant. Some kids with cancer need more than blood. They may also need a bone marrow transplant or organ transplant. This process is much more difficult than a transfusion, but it is also a way that someone else can share life and energy with you.

Have you ever had a transplant
or a transfusion?

Have you ever given blood for someone else?

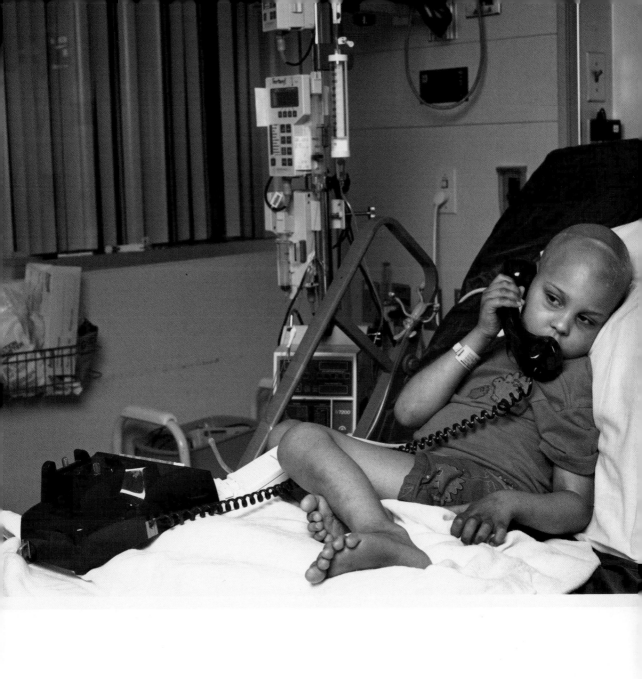

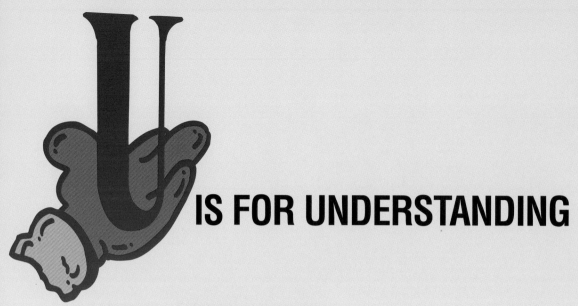

U IS FOR UNDERSTANDING

Because cancer can be
    a terrible and difficult thing,
    everybody needs
    lots and lots of understanding.

Take time to listen to the people around you.
Take time to talk about what you
    are thinking and feeling and doing.
Take time to make new friends.
Take time to celebrate old friends.

Understanding is a way of making
    the hard work of living with cancer
    a little easier.

Who is an understanding person in your life?

is for VISUALIZE

When I am very sick, I find it helpful
    to think about getting better.

I think about
    special things I like to do.
I paint imaginary pictures
    of beautiful places.
I dream about something wonderful
    that I am going to accomplish.
I imagine doing the things I do best.
I draw a picture of what it will be like
    when I don't have cancer anymore.

My mind is very powerful, and thinking good things
    will help me through the bad times.

What do you visualize
    when you are not feeling well?

What are the very
    best wishes you visualize?

W IS FOR WISHES

" I wish that people wouldn't make fun of me."
April, 12 yrs.

" I wish to have a family and seven children. "
Kristi, 16 yrs.

"I wish I could be a policeman and get all the bad guys."
Mark, 5 yrs.

"I wish I could run again."
Jennifer, 15 yrs.

"I wish I never had this cancer and could go to the park everyday."
Brandon, 6 yrs.

"I wish for a brand new bedroom."
Rachael, 11 yrs.

"My wish is to be able to live my life like I used to with my hair up and to not have to worry about my medications or what people think."
Kristi, 16 yrs.

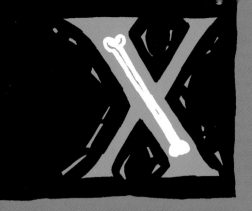 **is for X-RAYS**

When you have cancer,
    the doctor may need help to visualize and
        see what is happening inside your body.
            One way of seeing is to take
                an X-ray picture.

Another way is called a CAT scan.
    CAT scans take a little longer and
        are kind of noisy.

There are also MRI and PET scans.
    They take an even longer time
        and are very, very noisy.

So ask for ear plugs and relax,
    because none of these
        picture-taking things hurt.

And while you are lying there,
    you can make your own secret imaginary
    pictures that no machine can see.

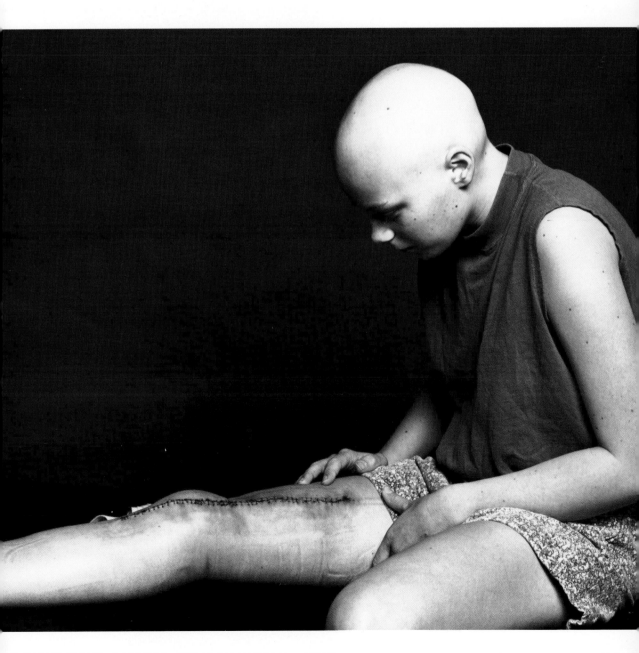

IS FOR YO-YO

When you have cancer, you sometimes feel like the yo-yo
on the end of a string.
Spinning up during the good days,
tumbling down on the bad days.

You learn to take things a day at a time.
You can never be sure
how you will feel tomorrow.

This can be very difficult.
It can also help slow us down
and help us appreciate
the life around us and in us.

Yo-yos are fun toys.
Walk the dog,
shoot the moon,
rock the cradle,
around the world.
Do you know these or any other
yo-yo tricks?

Do you ever have yo-yo days?

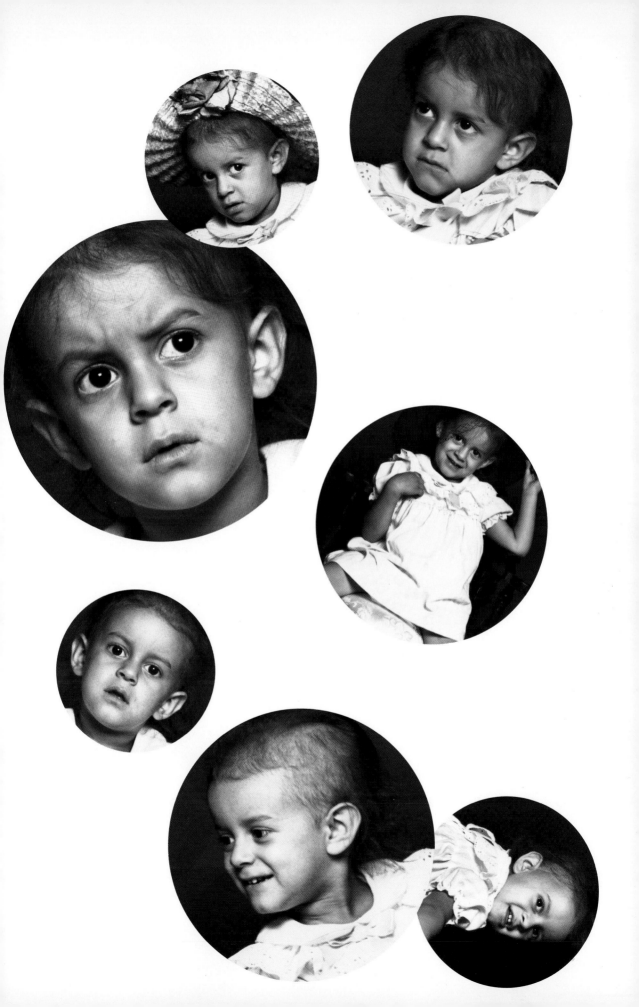

Z IS FOR ZOWEE!!!

Zowee!
is my favorite thing to yell on my good days.
Zowee!
You can yell it loud or sing it in a song.
Zowee!
You can whisper it to friends
and make them smile or laugh.
Zowee!

You can even make up your own special
good day words:
Zissle-zoks,
zingle,
zangle,
zookoidable,
zantastikable!!!!

I hope you will have lots of days
for laughing and making up words.

Fighting cancer makes you a
Zowee-Wowee kind of person!!!

Our Work

*T*he Children's Legacy creates and provides programs and materials which allow children with life-threatening illnesses to tell their stories of healing into wellness or passing into death. We assist them in creating their own legacy utilizing photography, writing and drawing to document feelings and thoughts associated with their illness.

The Children's Legacy provides all programs and services completely free of charge to those families choosing to participate. We are a small, nonprofit agency recognized as tax-exempt by the Internal Revenue Service. We are in need of ongoing financial support in order to keep this vision alive. Please help us by sending your tax-deductible donation:

The Children's Legacy
P.O. Box 300305
Denver, Colorado 80203
303.830.7595

Thank You

You are Invited
TO CREATE
Your Own Alphabet Book

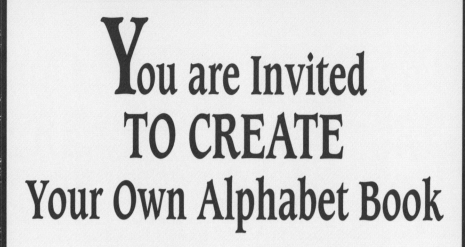

When: today, tomorrow, anytime, your time

Where: on the pages following

How: with paint, pencils, photos...
whatever inspires you

Why: Because
YOU ARE EXCEPTIONAL!!!!

RSVP: If you would like (we would like!),
please make a photocopy of one or more of
your created pages and send them to
The Children's Legacy, P.O. Box 300305
Denver, CO 80203 USA
303.830.7595

B

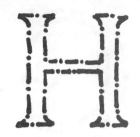

M

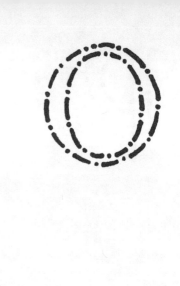

P

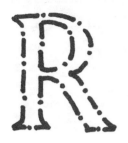

V

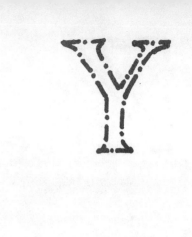